THE CHRISTIAN
WOMAN

Secrets to enjoying your marriage

PATRICIA SAPPOR

Foreword By: ARCHBISHOP NICHOLAS DUNCAN-WILLIAMS

THE CHRISTIAN WOMAN

For further information please contact:
P. O. Box CT 2606,Cantonments, Accra
Tel: +233(0)263000459
E-mail:patriciasappor@yahoo.com

ISBN: 9798352295724

Designed by: Indes Procom Ltd.
+233(0)264881018

Printed by:
Spearhead Consult P.O. Box
10728, Accra-North
+233(0)206500004

CONTENTS

DEDICATION

Dedicated with love to my dearest husband, Mr. Frederick Dornu Sappor, who has been an unshakeable pillar of support in my professional life and ministry.

He has made me a wife, a mother, an overcomer and brought out the best in me.

Honey, thank you for your love.

I love you.

ACKNOWLEDGMENTS

I will like to express my sincerest gratitude to my Spiritual Father, Archbishop Nicholas Duncan-Williams, founder and general overseer of Action Chapel International, who was the instrument God used to lead me to Christ and who has since fathered, mentored, discipled and taught me the Word of God, helping me build an unmatched capacity to pray.

I will like to thank the Leadership of Action Chapel International, especially Bishop James Saah, Bishop Nyarko Antwi, Bishop Ebenezer Obodai, Bishop Ben Anum and Bishop Isaac Clive Mould for their support and interest in my ministry and in my family.

I thank my parents, Mr. and Mrs. Andrews Adjetey Boye, of blessed memory, who, by their marriage and Christian lives, taught and demonstrated the true and practical Christian marriage which has helped my own walk through the journey of marriage.

I thank my children Wendell-Solomon, Paulynn and Frederick for their love and commitment to the family and to my ministry. I am proud of you all.

Thanks also go to my siblings for their love and support. God bless you all.

I thank my wonderful friends Mrs. Patience Ablorh Quarcoo, Mrs. Peggy Dzodzomenyo, Mrs. Rose Kpodo and Mrs. Alberta Okine for our great friendship of over four decades.

I thank all the Daughters of Zion Worldwide for their prayers especially Rev Irene Acquah Hayford, Rev. Olivia Dotse, Rev. Abigail Ocansey, Rev Doctor Aramansah Forjoe, Rev. Bose Ocansey, Min. Beatrice Darkwa for their support, encouragement and Love.

Many thanks also go to Mr. and Mrs. Charles Adjei, Rev. and Mrs. Koranteng Smart, Mrs. Freda Osafo and Dr. and Mrs. Philip Amekudzi for their love.

I acknowledge the help and support of Bishop Ebenezer Obodai, Reverend Patrick Otieku-Boadu, Pastor Dan Asafo Boakye, Miss Tina Boadi, Mr. Morgan Asiedu, Mrs. Esther Sahnoon and

Combert Impressions for bringing all the pieces together, editing this book and making it a reality.

Finally, to all others who have in diverse ways worked behind the scenes to make this a reality.

FOREWORD

And the LORD God said,

> *"It is not good that man should be alone;
> I will make him a helper comparable to
> him"*

> *(Genesis 2:18, NKJV).*

> *"And the Lord God caused a deep sleep to
> fall on Adam, and he slept; and He took
> one of his ribs, and closed up the flesh in
> its place. Then the rib which the Lord
> God had taken from man He made into a
> woman, and He brought her to the man.
> And Adam said: 'This is now bone of my
> bones And flesh of my flesh; She shall be
> called Woman, Because she was taken out
> of Man.' Therefore a man shall leave his
> father and mother and be joined to his
> wife, and they shall become one flesh."*

> *(Genesis 2:21-24, NKJV).*

Marriage is clearly God's idea. He decided that man needed a helper and provided one for him in His own way. We note how God promised a HELPER, created a WOMAN and finally introduced a WIFE to Adam. God's plan and purpose for marriage, just like God Himself, has not changed even though many marriages are not conforming to His original pattern. It is against this background that Rev. Mrs. Pat Sappor's contribution comes forth as a pointer to Divine Principles in Marriage, especially for women.

Rev. Mrs. Pat Sappor is one of my daughters in Ministry. She has served in different capacities here in the Action Chapel family over the years. She is a Banker, a Wife, a Mother, a Marriage Counsellor and an Ordained Minister.

In this book, ***THE CHRISTIAN WOMAN: Secrets to Enjoying Your Marriage,*** Rev. Mrs. Pat Sappor shares some very important biblical truths on Marriage. She draws from her rich professional experience and years in Ministry to help women position themselves for a happy marriage. She shares some personal testimonies to help throw more light on the topic. She introduces some important ingredients and secrets of marriage, emphasises some time-tested management principles and crowns it with some nuggets for married couples. It is scripture-based, beautifully written and enjoyable to read.

THE CHRISTIAN WOMAN: *Secrets to Enjoying Your Marriage* is a book you must read, especially as a woman, if you desire to understand your role in marriage and intend to enjoy your marriage. I encourage you to read it prayerfully and share the truths it puts forward with your family, friends and loved ones. Your life will not be the same.

ARCHBISHOP NICHOLAS DUNCAN-WILLIAMS

Founder, Action Chapel International

ENDORSEMENTS

Pat's book adds to the several books on marriage that have been written and she seems to have chosen very carefully areas that are very relevant to the times. She places great emphasis on those areas that are considered problematic and the joy I have about her book is the application of some relevant scriptures. Her style is quite different from other books that have been written, in that, she provides at the end of each chapter the highlights of the main points. It therefore makes it relatively easy for one to know what each chapter is all about.

Pat is a pastor at the Action Chapel International and my hope is that she will be an encouragement especially to the young who want direction and guidance as they seek peace and happiness in their marriages.

REV. S. OTU-PIMPONG
Senior Pastor, Legon Baptist Church

The family is the primary unit of society and the foundational pillar around which society is built. More than ever before, the institutions of family, parenthood and marriage are under siege. Many are searching for ideas on how to have successful and lasting marriages. In this book, ***The Christian woman: Secrets to enjoying your marriage***, Rev. Mrs. Patricia Sappor has drawn from her rich experiences as a Minister and a high level professional to package relevant lessons that every woman and anyone seeking divine direction for marriage can benefit from. I highly recommend this book.

REV. ALBERT OCRAN
Author, Minister &
Lead Consultant of Legacy & Legacy

Today's societal pressures and challenges render marriage a tough terrain to surmount. Rev. Mrs. Pat Sappor has shared her rich experiences and the lessons learnt thereof - experiences and lessons guided by the uncommon wisdom drawn from the deep wells of God's Word. She has also provided vital keys to help readers not only to navigate this mysterious construct but to also enjoy marriage just as God planned it.

Emma Amoo-Gottfried
Proprietress,
Faith Montessori School

Mrs. Sappor's book, THE CHRISTIAN WOMAN: Secrets to Enjoying Your Marriage, is very practical and speaks to the common issues that every marriage faces. It should help many marriages to stay on the right path and reduce the ratio of divorce in Christian marriages. Although written primarily for the Christian wife, the Christian husband can also learn a lot from the principles. I recommend it to all Christian couples both young and old.

MORGAN FIANKO ASIEDU
Executive Director,
Legal, Human Res. & Compliance
Ecobank Ghana Ltd.

Unto the Lord be the glory, great things He has done and greater things He will do. Amen. What more can I say than to bless the name of the Lord for this packaged answered prayer, THE CHRISTIAN WOMAN: Secrets To Enjoying Your Marriage.

I have thoroughly read this book and I can only describe it as an "answered prayer." It is simply a must own. It is your guide to that lifelong journey of blissful marriage that you so desire as a Christian woman. Hey! Our men can read too. After all, the two shall become one.

To the unmarried, you have the opportunity to make your marriage what it ought to be even before you get into it. Bible says in HOSEA 4:6 that, "My people are destroyed for lack of knowledge." Arm yourself with knowledge and do not go into the union of marriage unadvisedly. That is why I am grateful to God for the life of Rev. Pat Sappor for availing herself to be used as an instrument and a vessel of divine knowledge through her Godly-inspired book, THE CHRISTIAN WOMAN: Secrets To Enjoying Your Marriage.

All the secrets you need as a Christian woman to please God as a married woman, satisfy your husband through and through, be a blessing unto your children, remain a virtuous woman and fulfill your God-given destiny on earth is embedded in this book. If you patiently read this book and commit the pages to practice, all you will ever have to pray for is long life to keep enjoying all the many blessings there are in marriage.

To the already married, it is everything you know and more, it is everything you have not been doing that needs to be done, it is the answer to all the questions you have been asking in your marriage, and it is simply the turnaround to that blissful marriage you so desire. And if you think you are enjoying your marriage to the fullest, this book is what you need to enjoy it infinitely.

I simply recommend it to every Christian woman who has God, her marriage and her family as her priorities. You can never go wrong with THE CHRISTIAN WOMAN: Secrets To Enjoying Your Marriage.

Rev. Pat Sappor, God bless you richly and it is our prayer that you continue to avail yourself to be an inspiration to the world. To Mr. Sappor, we simply love and appreciate you.

EDEM KNIGHT-TAY
Host, "Home Affairs" (Joy 99.7Fm)
Proprietress, Evergreen Child Development Centre

01

INTRODUCTION

Having been married for decades, and surmounted some of the hurdles of marriage life and witnessed and heard some of the challenges that women sometimes face in their relationships, I felt burdened to share some secrets I have personally learnt from my own marriage that I am confident will yield tremendous results should they be applied to some of the situations many women face in their marriages.

After many years of marriage, I have come to realise that not being ignorant of the devices of the enemy is the strongest weapon the Christian Woman can have. The devices of the enemy are so subtle and ordinary that they can be ignored and never traced to the enemy.

It is easy for a spouse to become terribly annoyed or upset and focus on minor issues such as bad eating habits, poor sense of dressing and bad mannerisms. These trivial issues can be nurtured to create and cause what I call marital havoc. These are 'the little foxes' in marriage. Once such irritants are not nipped in the bud, other negative triggers begin to creep into the psyche and they can further degenerate into a downward cycle of negativity.

Somebody once shared with me a vision she had about a little misunderstanding in her relationship. In the vision, she saw a tiny worm in their home, which she could have killed by simply stepping on it. Later, she observed the worm growing through various stages, eventually becoming a huge and extremely agile snake moving everywhere in the house. Impossible to be captured and killed, the house became uninhabitable.

These 'little foxes' in marriages and relationships, if they are not handled properly from the outset, can transform into full-grown pythons, which can be very destructive to the relationship. This is why the apostle Paul, by the inspiration of the Holy Spirit, cautioned that:

> *"See to it that no one falls short of the grace of God and that no bitter root grows up to cause trouble and defile many."*
>
> *(Hebrews 12:15, NIV)*

The Book of Solomon foretold Paul's advice:

> *"Catch for us the foxes, the little foxes that ruin the vineyards, our vineyards that are in bloom."*

(Song of Solomon 2:15, NIV)

Divorce statistics are staggering in our world today. It is reported that over fifty percent of marriages fail in the United States and about thirty percent fail in Africa. *(Source–UN's Demographics and Social Statistics Division; Wikipedia, The free encyclopedia.)*

Have you ever observed some loving elderly couples and wondered how they did it and why they are still happy after so many years? Marriage is 'work' and it requires a lot of effort and sacrifice to maintain it.

God has designed marriage to be enjoyed just as the Church enjoys the blessings of God. This book will unearth some of the practical ways to sustain your marriage life, offering tips to help couples, especially women, improve their relationships and enjoy their marriages. I encourage all women to read this timely book and digest its contents.

02

THE ART OF MARRIAGE

Marriage is designed to bring total joy spiritually, emotionally and physically to both husband and wife, uniting them in a covenant relationship between themselves and their creator. I have a very strong conviction that God did not design marriage to be a perpetual union for sorrow and unhappiness. After decades of marriage life, I have come to understand the art of marriage on a daily basis through the ministration of the Holy Spirit, the study of the Word, personal experiences and those of other couples. On a continuous basis, I try to change my ways even though sometimes I forget and do certain things I have resolved not to. As Christians, we clearly know that the first miracle Jesus performed was at a marriage ceremony where He turned water into wine.

> *"On the third day there was a wedding in Cana of Galilee, and the mother of Jesus was there. Now both Jesus and His disciples were invited to the wedding."*
>
> *(John 2:1-2, NKJV)*

As we know from the story, there was a shortage of wine though Jesus was at the ceremony. Jesus' attention was drawn to the problem and He fixed the problem by turning water into wine. The fact that Jesus Christ is in our marriages does not absolve us from marital problems, but there is one assurance that when we turn to Him in difficult times, He will fix the problems in our marriages.

The tastelessness of water being turned into something very sweet at a marriage ceremony depicts God's plans for us concerning marriage. His wish is that we enjoy the sweetness of our marriages just as we enjoy the sweetness of wine. We see from the story that water was turned into wine as a result of simple obedience. Mary said to the disciples in John 2:5 (NKJV): ***"Whatever He says to you, do it."***

I am not yet aware of marriages that do not have challenges, but I am aware of many marriages that have surmounted the challenges through prayer, the Holy Spirit and obedience to the Word of God.

One of the key requirements of the Christian woman in a marriage relationship is submission. Submitting to your husband's leadership in marriage can be difficult but this can be made easy if you ask the Holy Spirit to help you. Sometimes it is very difficult to submit when you are not in agreement with a decision or comfortable with a particular action taken by the man of the house.

Though I love my husband very much, from the outset it was not easy at all for me to submit in some areas of our marriage simply because we came from completely different backgrounds. It was a herculean task. Although I was born again and spirit-filled, I did not see why my husband wanted and expected me to perform certain household chores when we had agreed before marriage that those duties would be performed by our domestic help. I felt deceived and extremely upset. I simply was not amused performing those chores. This was a major challenge and a threat to our young marriage. I asked God several questions and asked myself if it was really the will of God for us to get married.

I had made the mistake of focusing on the perceived deception rather than on the Word of God, and this affected me emotionally, psychologically and physically. My expectations were dashed and I wished I could turn the clock backwards. This 'little fox' or worm began growing in our relationship, which was less than six months old. Thank God I did not wait for it to transform into a full-blown, uncontrollable python. My frustration, anger and doubt one day brought me to my knees. In prayer, the Holy Spirit ministered to me and referred me to Ephesians 5:22 (KJV), which states: *"Wives, submit yourselves unto your own husbands, as unto the Lord."*

It was painful to come to terms with the reality of Ephesians 5:22. But I had no choice but to obey the Word of God and do as my husband expected, however reluctantly. This brought joy and peace to our home.

> *"Wives, submit yourselves to your own husbands as you do to the Lord. For the husband is the head of the wife as Christ*

is the head of the church, his body, of which he is the Savior. Now as the church submits to Christ, so also wives should submit to their husbands in everything."

(Ephesians 5:22-24, NIV)

This is a powerful scripture, which can yield amazing results in relationships. In the marriage ceremony in Canaan, the water was turned into wine through obedience.

The story of Naaman also clearly demonstrates the power of submission and obedience. As told in 2 Kings 5:10-14, Naaman was too proud to humble himself and submit to the instruction of the prophet Elisha given through his servant Gehazi. Yet, when he later submitted and did as he was told, he received his healing.

Key Learning Points

- *What I learnt from the beginning of my marriage was to submit to my husband.*

- *There are enough legitimate and justifiable reasons for women not to submit to their husbands, but one of the keys to unlocking our joy and peace in our marriages is submission.*

- *I have learnt that genuine submission opens doors.*

- *Submission can sometimes be difficult but we must conform to God's word.*

- *It is important that when judging our husbands and getting upset over some of the things they do, women must, first of all, assess themselves to see if their acts are in accordance with the Word of God.*

- *The Holy Spirit's counsel and continuous reading of the Word of God will ease the difficulty in submission.*

- *Just as Christ loves us even when we do not show Him gratitude for what He did for us, so are we still called to put our husbands first even when their love is not so perfect. Love covers a multitude of sins and, in some days to come, it may be your husband who loves his not-so-grateful wife.*

03

THE INGREDIENTS FOR MARRIAGE

One of the most difficult tasks to take on in life is the commitment to live with another person. For many people, it is one of the best things they ever did and for others one of the hardest things they could think of. We go into marriage with such high hopes and expectations of everlasting goodness and bliss. Then the reality of day-to-day living sets in, along with financial challenges, cultural shocks, individual idiosyncrasies and different ways of doing things. The situation is compounded with the addition of children.

A healthy appetite does not guarantee great tasting food. Furthermore, a bad tasting food can kill every bit of appetite one might have had for the food initially. No matter how high your expectations are for a meal, you will need the right ingredients, recipe and cooking experience to make the food taste good. Likewise, in marriage you need the right ingredients to guarantee harmony and order to get the relationship working.

The key driving forces of marriage are 'love' and 'purpose.' Now, one may ask, what is the purpose of

God for women when they enter into marriage? The answer is to be a help meet. If men (or our husbands) had it all, they would not have needed help and God wouldn't have seen the need to bring in the woman.

My understanding of the word 'help' is the deliberate effort to assist. Sometimes the helper may have more than the person who needs the help. Women are naturally endowed with lots of gifts and are expected to demonstrate these gifts to their husbands in their quest for more of those very gifts.

For example, women by nature know love, which is a gift from God to them. In desiring love to be demonstrated by their husbands, women need to exhibit the love they know in order to derive more. I believe wholeheartedly in what the Bible says in Ephesians 5:25 (NKJV). *"Husbands, love your wives, just as Christ also loved the church and gave Himself for her."* For the Bible to demand this of husbands is an indication that it could be an area of challenge for men.

My experience in marriage has taught me that all the ingredients of marriage are embedded in love. The purpose of women being help meet to their husbands is to support and demonstrate to them how the gifts and qualities bestowed on women will be of benefit to the family. Whilst I empathise with many women who have demonstrated impeccable godly characters yet their marital expectations are not fulfilled, I wish to say that it should become a way of life. It should be part of you.

The following six (6) attributes are among the many that help to foster strong marital union, especially at the early stages of living together as husband and wife. They are the pillars of post-marriage adjustment.

Love

The journey of marriage can only be sustained with genuine love for God and for the marriage. Love gives you the ability and capacity to accommodate the weaknesses of your spouse. Love is about giving.

You cannot love without giving. God demonstrated His love for us by giving.

> *"For God so loved the world that He gave…."*
>
> *(John 3:16)*

> *"Above all, love each other deeply, because love covers over a multitude of sins."*
>
> *(1Peter 4:8, NIV)*

> *"…God is love. Whoever lives in love lives in God, and God in them."*
>
> *(1John 4:16, NIV)*

Joy

The Christian Woman, even in difficult times, can always live in joy when she continuously connects with the Father because true joy is found only in God. One can only be joyful when one trusts in the Lord, knowing that our God is faithful. You can live in Joy and please God continuously through faith.

"And without faith it is impossible to please God…."

(Hebrews 11:6, NIV)

Peace

Peace within the heart of the Christian Woman guarantees her focus in the marriage. It is very easy to see, hear or experience disturbing news or situations in a relationship. As difficult as the situation is, the contented Christian Woman should be able to say: *"Though the fig tree does not bud and there are no grapes on the vines, though the olive crop fails and the fields produce no food, though there are no sheep in the pen and no cattle in the stalls, yet I will rejoice in the Lord, I will be joyful in God my Savior. The Sovereign Lord is my strength; he makes my feet like the feet of a deer, he enables me to tread on the heights." (Habakkuk 3:17-19, NIV)*

Endurance

Life without challenges ceases to be life. Challenges are part and parcel of our lives as human beings. Similarly, challenges abound in marriages. The Christian Woman should have the capacity to endure the challenges of the marriage and make a commitment and determination to overcome through the Blood. *"But thanks be to God! He gives us the victory through our Lord Jesus Christ." (1 Corinthians 15:57, NIV)*

When we endure, we learn from the challenges, prepare, position ourselves for ultimate victory in the future and become beneficial to society. From Hebrews 5:8, remember that Christ learnt obedience through the suffering He suffered and being made perfect, He became the author of eternal salvation.

Understanding

The Bible clearly admonishes husbands to dwell with their wives in knowledge and understanding. As women, we are so complex and complicated, hence God's instructions to men. I have also come to realise that understanding the expectations and desires of the man is a woman's most priceless possession.

In the book of Esther, we learn of Queen Vashti who lost her position as a wife and a queen because she was disrespectful to the king. If Queen Vashti knew and understood how important respect was to King Ahasuerus or any other man, I believe she would have complied with the request of the king.

Respect for each other

Every single individual wants his or her esteem enhanced every time. Accordingly, giving each other respect in the relationship is a sure catalyst for sustaining the marriage. It is necessary to demonstrate respect for each other and not to take each other for granted. Complacency in a marriage relationship is a sure recipe for a reduction in admiration and confidence. Romans 12:10 (NIV) reminds us to "Be kindly affectionate to one another with brotherly love, in honor giving preference to one another."

> *"But the fruit of the Spirit is love, joy, peace, longsuffering, gentleness, goodness, faith."*
>
> *(Galatians 5:22, KJV)*

These attributes are the foundation upon which the marriage will be built. Remember that Jesus spoke about the need to build on a solid foundation, else one risks being ridiculed and mocked by others.

> *"He is like a man which built an house, and digged deep, and laid the foundation on a rock: and when the flood arose, the stream beat vehemently upon that house, and could not shake it: for it was founded upon a rock."*
>
> *(Luke 6:48, KJV)*

I have come to realise that just as different fruits and plants have varying gestation and harvest periods, these attributes take varying periods to be learnt and applied by husbands and wives. Today, many married couples expect immediate companionship and intimacy without investing time and effort in building the relationship and making known their expectations of each other. When expectations are not shared with each other, disillusionment may probably become an everyday experience.

In my marital relationship, I had so many expectations of my husband. I was expecting to be pampered a lot, to be told 'I love you always, to be showered with gifts, my husband not being upset and experiencing unending times of happiness and joy. Even though my husband fulfilled these expectations to some extent, and there was no question about his love for me, I realised I did not feel pampered and loved enough. Sometimes I was unhappy, not because he had offended me but simply because in my own mind I had my own expectations of how I wanted to be treated.

The Bible says in Luke 6:38 (NKJV): *"Give and it will be given to you: good measure, pressed down, shaken together and running over will be put into your bosom. For with the same measure that you use, it will be measured back to you."*

This scripture is often quoted as a universal principle of giving both in-cash and in-kind, especially during fundraising. However, it is wholly applicable to the relationship between a man and a woman in marriage. As a Christian wife, you must remember that you are a help meet. You have to meet the needs of your husband. You have what your husband does not have and therefore give what you have to complement what he has and supplement what he lacks.

I took the initiative to give my husband a kiss and say I love you every morning after we pray. By so doing, I am now also receiving in good measure, pressed down, shaken together and running over. And this has become a daily ritual.

Key Learning Points

- *Men do not have it all and God has given women what it takes to support them to be total.*

- *Women are help meets to their husbands.*

- *Women need to give out what they have in order to receive in good measure of what they expect.*

- *The expectations of women will be met when they invest and sow the seeds of what they have into their husbands in order to harvest over and above what they expect.*

04

THE SECRETS TO ENJOYING YOUR MARRIAGE

There are practical ways to enjoy your marriage physically, socially, spiritually and financially. I will share with you some practical tools I have used to achieve great results in my marriage.

Staying physically attractive to your husband, comporting yourself psychologically, spiritually and financially must not be taken for granted.

Physical

Every day, I gain new insight and understanding regarding the basics of marriage. Men are attracted by what they see. They are sight species. My husband never complained about my style of dressing, but one day whilst shopping for some general items for the home, he selected some interesting lingerie for me. I was shocked but did not express it immediately. I had always assumed that he did not like such things. It taught me the lesson that a man is a man in just the same way that women are typically emotional beings. If husbands do not get what they want in the home, they will go and get it somewhere else.

"Do not desire her beauty in your heart,
nor let her catch you with her eyelids."
(Proverbs 6:25, NASB)

There is a good lesson to learn from this scripture. The Bible admonishes men not to go after or desire the beauty of other women apart from their wives. Women are naturally made to look beautiful and attractive but there is always the possibility that your husband will desire another woman. There is a strong need or desire in every man, so it is the responsibility of the woman to meet that need by looking beautiful and desirable for her husband at all times. By so doing, the strong attraction and desire in your man would be directed towards you. Catch the attention of your man and let him desire your beauty. Beauty also means you must be neat and inviting. Keep your hair, teeth, toes, and fingers tidy and attractive. Wear the right attire at the right time.

Be current with fashion and try to do the same thing differently by being creative and innovative at home, especially behind closed doors with your husband. Avoid doing the same thing the same way all the time. In the book of Esther in the Old Testament, we learn of the lengthy beautifying process candidates for the queenship position underwent.

> *"Before a young woman's turn came to go in to King Xerxes, she had to complete twelve months of beauty treatments prescribed for the women, six months with oil of myrrh and six with perfumes and cosmetics."*
>
> *(Esther 2:12, NIV)*

Looks do matter. Making time for your body can make a real difference in your relationship with others and especially with your husband.

I have realised that, in as much as men perhaps generally do not have to come out openly that they admire trends or fashion, they secretly like it. I was chatting with a male friend of mine and he told me that anytime he sees another woman wearing something that he is attracted to and admires, he tries to get his wife that same thing. Longevity in marriage is no license for complacency neither is it a guarantee for 'till death do us part.'

It is therefore important to be abreast with current fashion trends, but it should be done carefully as Christians. We should be very fashionable but modest as Christian mothers and wives. We should bear in mind that not only are we dressing to feel good about ourselves but also to make our husbands feel proud and confident about us, while also conforming to the decency and morality that the Bible places on us. It's a multi-faceted dynamics.

Before I got married, I used to like a particular colour and certain types of dresses and accessories. My fiancé was not too thrilled, excited and fascinated about this sense of fashion, so I changed even though I could have stubbornly stuck to what I liked. There should always be a point of compromise or convergence for the man and woman when making choices. Usually, you need to agree with each other to make the two

of you happy. This is in line with scripture. *"Can two walk together, except they be agreed?"*
(Amos 3:3, KJV)

A woman once told me that whenever she dresses and her husband is pleased with her style of dressing, she does not really bother or worry about what other people say. She proudly said: "I dress to my husband's taste."

The fundamental thing to remember is that you are in a marriage that should generate enduring happiness for both of you. Consequently, it is obligatory that you strive to keep each other happy. The two of you need to agree on what makes you very happy.

I have realised that whenever my husband returns home from work he is looking for surprises because many a time, by the time he comes back home, I have done something new which really amuses and brings him joy. Surely, men like surprises. Adam was asleep and when he woke up, he had a surprise from God–Eve. Husbands may not express it even though they enjoy and appreciate it very much. Wives should try to be innovative and do new things. Men easily get bored and are always eager to explore.

I strongly believe that is why some men look around and go out chasing other attractions. As a Christian wife, you must try to add variety by polishing up the old things to become new. I often change the bed sheets to yellow, white, or, at times, pink. These are all invitations to add colour to your marriage. The more the interaction you have with him, even by way of closeness, the better the strength of the relationship. As a woman, I believe these are all avenues to get your husband to stay closer to you.

Men also like clean environments and tidy women. The first aspect of cleanliness should start from the home, right from the gate to the living room, kitchen, bedroom and every other room in the house. All these add up to the relationship. Usually, men may not express their feelings to you even when they appreciate it. Women should therefore not be discouraged when the compliments do not come; men appreciate, admire and enjoy them in private.

> *"Men do not despise a thief, if he steals to satisfy his soul when he is hungry;...."*
>
> *(Proverbs 6:30, KJV)*

When a thief steals to satisfy his hunger, the Bible says he should not be despised or blamed. When you make your husband starve or hungry, he will go and steal from somewhere else, and if he does, you may not have the moral right to despise or blame him because you had the food and did not give him.

God gave me this revelation about sex. That sex in marriage is like food to a man, so if a wife uses sex as punishment, especially when he offends her and she deprives him, he will be hungry and starve and the result may be that he dines elsewhere.

Social

I believe that the Pareto Principle, which talks about the 80/20 rule, is quite credible and applicable to every facet of our lives. In your life, only 20% of the people around you provide 80% of your needs. That is, 80% of your needs are provided by only 20% of the people around you. You need to identify this 20% because that is where your social life fits. In times of challenges, you will notice that 80% of the support needed will come from the 20%. It is therefore important to always identify the 20% and know how much time and energy to invest in them. This subject is handled in depth in chapter 5 under Time Management.

Your husband and children are supposed to be part of the 20% that generate 80% of the satisfaction and assistance you need. Therefore, since they are the closest of your social net, it is your singular duty to make them happy. If you are not deriving as much as 80% social capital from 20% of the people around you, of which your husband and children are a part, then there is a need to redefine your focus and priorities. Socially, you need to know where your bread is buttered.

Different social interests, which at times are sharply in contrast with each other, cause many rifts in marriages. It is prudent also to be interested in the social interest of your spouse. I was not interested in politics but because my husband has a strong interest in politics, I have also developed interest in it. I had to because that is one of the issues or topics that bring us into many discussions together. Anytime he comes home he tells me what is in the newspapers politically; thus, I am compelled to be interested. My interest in the things of God, on the other hand, also generates many spiritual and interactive discussions.

Spiritual

A Christian wife must be an intercessor for her husband. I believe women are more open to the things of God than men and therefore I would want to put the responsibility of intercession on the woman. Even though my husband is prayerful, I know one of my assignments as a Christian wife is intercession and God is using me more and more to intercede for the family. Hannah, the Shunamite woman, Abigail, Miriam and Deborah, to name just a few, were great women of prayer who stood in the gap and interceded for the salvation of their home, family and nation. The role of a Christian Woman in a family cannot be underestimated. You can be sure that her spiritual directions, if she is in tune with God, will go a long way to sustain the family.

> *"Take hold of shield and buckler, and stand up for mine help."*
>
> *(Psalm 35:2, KJV)*

If you remember the story in Ezekiel 37, God asked Ezekiel to prophesy to 'the valley of dry bones,' and as he was prophesying, the following happened:

> *"There was a noise, and behold a shaking, and the bones came together, bone to his bone. And when I beheld, lo, the sinews and the flesh came up upon them, and the skin covered them above: but there was no breath in them."*
>
> *(Ezekiel 37:7–8, KJV)*

Note that every stage of the dry bones coming back to life was directed by prophesy. These, I believe, indicate levels of prayer. As women, we need to pray continuously to go beyond the noise level, rattling noise, bones coming together level and the flesh formation level. You cannot stop at the noise level or the rattling noise level. You cannot stop at the flesh formation level. It is midway, and you cannot even stop when everything has come together because after the whole body came together it was still dead. There was no breath in it.

Ezekiel could see the body there but there was no life in it until God told him to prophesy again to the four winds for breath to come.

> *"Then said he unto me, Prophesy unto the wind, prophesy, son of man, and say to the wind, thus saith the Lord God; Come from the four winds, O breath, and breathe upon these slain, that they may live. So I prophesied as he commanded me, and the breath came into them, and they lived, and stood up upon their feet, an exceeding great army."*
>
> *(Ezekiel 37:9–10, KJV)*

Therefore, it calls for serious and continuous intercession to change situations and pull down strongholds. Ephesians 6:8 says we should pray at all times and pray with all manner of prayer.

I was once called upon to share a few words with some women. I was fully prepared and ready to speak, but when I took the microphone, I felt a strong burden to travail, so I engaged all the women and turned the session into a prayer meeting. That night, on my bed, the Holy Spirit prompted me to continue praying. I started praying at 'noise level,' 'rattling noise level,' and then God instructed me to get up and move up to the next level.

Therefore, I got up and continued praying. Perhaps in my mind I got to the 'flesh level moved to the 'whole body level and the prayer became intense. As I continued praying, something happened in the spirit realm. At 2:00am, I went to bed. Thirty minutes later, armed robbers attempted to invade our home but they were unsuccessful.

There are of course so many distractions in marriage but my wish is that every Christian Woman, married and unmarried, will develop a way to focus and make intercessory prayer a way of life. God will certainly lighten the burden. Regular reading of the Word and walking in the Word of God will contribute immensely to the success of your marriage.

In one of my joyful and intensive worship moments, in the presence of the Lord, I said to God: "My Father, I do not know how I can describe you. You are everywhere, you are omnipresent and you are God." You know what God said? He said: "Everything that you see, everything that I have created, I am in it. I am there and my presence is in there."

So, if God created the sun and the moon, then He is present in them. So, what God is saying is that His creation represents His presence in things both in heaven and on the earth. My advice to women is that seeking the things of the Spirit should be their priority because it is more real than anything tangible. We are help meets to men and this suggests that men are deficient in some ways and we have to adequately fill that empty space. The person who is coming to help may even be stronger than the person who needs help. Therefore, we have been called to be helpers to our husbands. For this reason, if the woman looks at the deficiency of the man and she does not do what she is supposed to do, then she is not fulfilling the purpose of God in the marriage. We need to pray and read the Word of God, practise it and demonstrate it to our husbands.

Financial

Being a help meet to one's husband cuts across every area of the relationship. God never specified a particular area or areas where women ought to give help. It therefore presupposes that in every area of the man's life, the woman must provide support to make him complete i.e. physically, socially, spiritually and financially.

I have come to realise that women have a lot more financial opportunities than men. There are certain business opportunities that women can naturally engage in more easily than men. As a Chartered Banker, I still make time to generate other income through petty trading. A virtuous woman is one who uses her hands to generate more income.

I have interacted with many men who lament the financial burden that is upon them because there is no financial support from their wives.

> *"She considers a field and buys it; out of her earnings she plants a vineyard. She sets about her work vigorously; her arms are strong for her tasks. She sees that her trading is profitable, and her lamp does not go out at night. In her hand she holds the distaff and grasps the spindle with her fingers."*
>
> *(Proverbs 31:16–19, NIV)*

When wives take steps to generate extra income for the home, they enjoy the following benefits:

- *Meeting financial needs of the home.*
- *Meeting the financial needs of the Kingdom of God.*

- *Being an asset rather than a liability.*
- *Meeting the needs of the children.*
- *Gains a sense of self-worth and respect.*
- *Commands respect from husband and others.*
- *Ability to support others when in need.*
- *Makes her financially independent should the man be unavailable or unable to provide.*

However, financial wealth does not negate God's command for the wife to submit to her husband. Women should therefore be mindful of the fact that no matter how financially sound or blessed they are or become, they should be careful never to consciously or unconsciously ever assume the leadership role in the home, nor should they ever use their wealth as a source of punishment to the man.

My husband has always encouraged me to be financially successful and he has resolved to help me to be financially independent. This is extremely important, as one person should be able to support the other at any point in time. Ideally, no partner in marriage should be the sole breadwinner. Many women have become destitute because when they lost their husbands or their husbands were out of employment, the family could not stand. Their husbands had been the sole breadwinners. You should be able as a woman to generate some income and save some money for a 'rainy day.' Your husband may be rich but you should also be able to build some resources of your own.

It is necessary to be mindful of how you handle the wealth you acquire. As a woman, when God blesses you financially, do not use that as a rod to chastise your husband. It is not prudent for you to make it public that your husband is unable to provide and that you are the sole breadwinner of the family. A woman's glory is derived from her husband, so when you expose the financial and other weaknesses of your husband you are, in effect, belittling yourself. We have to support our husbands. Any legitimate means or source of income generation that a woman can secure to add to the family's kitty should not be discounted.

As wives, we must not be wasteful. We are created to be assets and not liabilities in our marriages. We need to be mindful of what we buy. We must cut out frivolous spending. If I want to buy jewelry, I will rather buy gold jewelry than a cheaper version such as copper jewelry that will corrode and lose its economic value in days. There is actually no wear and tear when it comes to articles of gold. We must constantly monitor the household budget to cut out needless expenses and reduce waste.

Always remember that financial transparency injects trust and honesty into the marriage relationship. A woman must endeavour to be financially transparent to her spouse as much as possible and practicable.

Key Learning Points

- *Men secretly admire and love fashion.*

- *Though inner beauty is a basic requirement of the Christian Woman, ignoring outward beauty could cost you your marriage.*

- *Deliberately create time to be with your husband and family, for they constitute the 20% that fulfills 80% of your needs.*

- *You are the goalkeeper of the family. Never cease praying and interceding for your family.*

- *Your prayers will always protect, deliver and bring joy and prosperity to the marriage and the family.*

- *Always find legitimate means to generate income for yourself. This will enhance your self-worth and give you an aura of success.*

05

THE ART OF MANAGEMENT IN MARRIAGE

"And God is able to make all grace abound toward you, that you, always having all sufficiency in all things, may have an abundance for every good work."

(2 Corinthians 9:8, NKJV)

Being a career woman, a wife and someone who is deeply involved in church activities, managing these roles needed a certain level of grace. At a point, I literally lived in the air, traveling from one country to another on official assignments. My husband understood the nature of my job and gave me every support needed. However, I knew certain gaps needed to be filled. On one of my trips, I changed my return date twice. The next time I called, my husband said: "I hope you are not going to change the date again." I realised my husband was giving me all the support he needed to but his desire was to have me around him most of the time.

Church activities were also a key attraction and a magnetic force in my life. I enjoyed and felt fulfilled in serving the Lord by being involved in church activities. I wanted to teach in Sunday school, be a counselor, a preacher and serve in the women's fellowship. The little time available after work was just not enough to handle the different activities I desired to do in the church.

My husband lovingly challenged me, asking, "How can you be doing everything in the church?" Again he said: "Honey, I know you love God but remember you need to give me some special attention." I sat back and realised that my husband will be happier if I gave him more time and attention.

Time Management

Women are expected to engage in motherly, wifely, social, spiritual and extended family duties, and are expected to give maximum attention to all these areas. Consequently, many women become typically overworked and exhausted.

In the book of Judges, Chapters 4-9, we learn of Deborah.

Deborah's profile

- She was the fourth and only female Judge in Israel.
- She led Israel for forty years.
- She had special abilities as a mediator, adviser and counselor.
- She was able to plan, direct and delegate when called upon to lead.
- She was a prophetess.
- She was a writer of songs.
- She was married to Lapidoth.
- She did not allow her profession and family life to come into conflict.

One of the keys to Deborah's effectiveness, in addition to her spiritual commitment and walk with God, was how she managed her time. Managing an entire household and keeping everything organised takes a lot of effort and sacrifice.

Deborah was a judge, the first female "Supreme Court" judge. She judged Israel for 40 years. She was a wife, a mother and a prophetess. The question is, how did she successfully manage all these roles? The answer lies in proper management of time.

When you know how to manage your time, you gain more control over whatever you want to do and achieve. Effectively managing your time will help you to choose what to work on and when. It ensures that you do the right thing at the right time. This is essential if you are to achieve anything of real value. For many, it seems as though there is just not enough time in the day to get everything done.

Some basic facts about time:

- Time is today's most valuable commodity.
- Time is money.
- Time is ultimately the most valuable resource.
- Time is perishable.
- Time is intangible.
- Time cannot be stored up for use later.

> *"Therefore we also, since we are surrounded by so great a cloud of witnesses, let us lay aside every weight,*

and the sin which so easily ensnares us, and let us run with endurance the race that is set before us."

(Hebrews 12:1, NKJV)

The race that is set before us can only be run within time. You cannot run the race outside of time. So, for the purposes of this topic, I consider anything that wastes our time, making us not have enough time, as the "weight and the sin" that can easily entangle us. Time management is simply getting the most out of the limited time you have to finish the race that is set before you. The race can be financial, social, economic, and so on. To effectively manage your time, the following should be taken into consideration:

- Identifying your mission.
- Planning and setting goal.
- Managing yourself.
- Managing other people.
- Getting results.

> *"Be very careful, then, how you live not as unwise but as wise, making the most of every opportunity, because the days are evil. Therefore do not be foolish, but understand what the Lord's will is."*
>
> *(Ephesians 5:15-17, NIV)*

Redeeming lost time

Time slips from us easily, yet we are called upon to focus our energy towards building a sense of discipline with respect to time consciousness. Save all you can for the best purposes by buying back or redeeming time through adjustment and priority rating.

1. Determine your mission

Set aside time to think about what you have to do within the day or within a week, month, quarter or year and write them down, if it is possible. That is, plan every activity you intend doing ahead of time.

Ask yourself these questions:

- What do I want to achieve?
- When do I want to achieve them?
- How do I achieve them?

2. Set goals

After determining your mission, you need to set goals. They may be short, medium or long-term goals. They can be daily, weekly, monthly or yearly goals.

If you do not have a clear sense of where you are headed just yet, you will not be able to plan how to get there. Your use of time should be organised to maximise the chances of achieving your set goals. Goals should be 'SMART' They must be Specfic, Measurable, Achievable, Realistic and Time bound.

3. Set out your own priorities

Priorities are those activities that have the right of precedence. It is the allotment of your time to do the most important things first. This should include only those activities that make a significant contribution to what you are trying to achieve, that is, 'your mission,' 'your goal' as well as the period within which to achieve it.

Be disciplined in identifying real priorities. Priorities are, by definition, the few critical or essential tasks rather than the many tasks.

Ask yourself these questions:

- What goals are the most important for me to achieve?
- When do I want to achieve them?

4. Plan

There is a saying that 'failing to plan is planning to fail.' Planning involves how you set your goals and how you can achieve those goals within the time you have set.

Ask yourself these questions again:

- What do I want to achieve?
- How do I achieve them?

Vilfredo Pareto, an Italian economist, discovered the Pareto Principle in 1897 when he observed that 80 percent of the land in England and every country he subsequently studied was owned by only 20% of the population. Through this observation and other analyses, he theorised that 80% of the results we generate come from 20% of the effort we put in. It is now a proven fact that about 20% of our planned efforts generate 80% of the results. In business, it is said that 80% of your revenue comes from 20% of your customers.

It is important therefore to identify the 20% of the people in our lives and also the 20% of the things we need to do to produce 80% of our needs. Our families obviously fall within the 20% of the people we need to focus on.

5. Managing interruptions

Most people do have their time interrupted through phone calls, information requests, urgent demands from friends and family members and a host of events that crop up unexpectedly. Social media has now become a magnetic force taking a chunk of our attention.

All these create inundated burdens on us, sometimes creating a lot of anxiety and stress. Some of these time consumers need to be dealt with immediately, whilst others need to be deferred or avoided. One needs wisdom to sort them out.

What should you do? Distinguish between what is 'Important' and what is 'Urgent.'

Important activities have outcomes that lead to the achievement of your overall goals i.e. *"the race set before you."* These are the activities I call 'Active Tasks.'
Urgent activities demand immediate attention and are usually associated with the achievement of someone else's goals, an uncomfortable problem or a situation that needs to be resolved. I call these 'Reactive Tasks.'

Unfortunately, Urgent activities are often the ones we rather concentrate on. They demand instant attention because the consequences of not dealing with them are immediate. However, they do not form a core part of what we have planned to do in a given period.

To manage your time effectively, you need to spend more time on the things that are Important and less time on the things that are Urgent but not important to you.

Ask yourself the following questions:

- Is this Important?
- Is it Urgent?
- Do I need to do it now?
- Can I defer it?
- Can I delegate?
- Will it contribute to the 80% of what I want to achieve in a day, month or year, socially and spiritually, etc.?

For activities that are both urgent and important such as resolving a dispute with your husband, taking a sick child to the hospital – ***Do them immediately.***

For important but not urgent things such as health and wellness screening – *Plan to do.*

For urgent but not important things, e.g. an impromptu request from a friend who is not in your 20% – *Spend minimal time or diplomatically decline or delegate if possible.*

For those activities that are neither urgent nor important, e.g. gossiping – *Avoid or cease.*

The "weight" and "sin" referred to in Hebrews 12:1 are what I call the time wasters. They are the things that distract you from your main objectives.

Time wasters	Time savers
Worries	Believing and praying
Unanticipated interruptions that contribute little to your goals.	Committing issues to God
Not prioritising	Multi-tasking
Poor planning and lack of contingency plans	Spending less time on reactive tasks

Time wasters	Time savers
Spending too much time on urgent but not important tasks	Establishing daily, short, medium and long term goals
Failing to delegate	Setting aside time for reflection
Staying at functions and ceremonies for a long and unplanned period of time	Defining your major projects and sticking to them to make you more productive
Piece meal shopping and cooking	Delegating/Planned shopping and cooking
Procrastinating	Planning and taking action on those plans

Jesus' Ministry and Time Management

Our Lord Jesus Christ understood Time Management and ensured that He managed His time well because He had a purpose to fulfill. The Bible tells us in 1John 3:8 (NKJV):

> *"For this purpose the Son of God was manifested, that He might destroy the works of the devil."*

Being conscious of disruptions and interruptions, Jesus woke up early in the morning and went to a solitary place to pray.

> *"Now in the morning, having risen a long while before daylight, He went out and departed to a solitary place and there He prayed."*
>
> *(Mark 1:35, NKJV)*

> *"And when He had sent the multitudes away, He went up on the mountain by Himself to pray. Now when evening came, He was alone there."*
>
> *(Matthew 14:23, NKJV)*

Jesus was able to manage His time well by identifying what was Urgent and what was Important. He knew exactly what needed to be done and at what time. The Bible tells us in John 11 that when Lazarus died, Jesus was informed. Even though it was urgent for Jesus to come when Lazarus died, it was not as important as what He was doing at that time, so

He had to sort out the more important thing before going to see to Lazarus.

Ordinarily, you and I would have left whatever we were doing and run to be with Mary and Martha. But Jesus knew He had to attend to the more important task first. Please, bear in mind that Jesus, of course, also wanted to prove to all that He could pray to the Father and the lifeless body would come back to life.

As outlined in Hebrews 12:1, there is a race set before each and everyone of us and that race can only be completed within Time. Thus, there is the need to manage and possibly redeem the time to accomplish our goals and fulfill our purposes.

Jesus made time to:
- Listen to people
- Study the Word of God though He was the Word
- Be alone with God praying
- Meet various physical needs

- Meet spiritual needs by teaching
- Teach others and make them disciples.

Since we are admonished to be imitators of Christ, it is our responsibility to walk in wisdom and redeem the time as Colossians 4:5 (NKJV) advises:

> *"Walk in wisdom toward those who are outside, redeeming the time."*

Jesus made good choices and we need to be responsible enough to learn from His example and make good choices regarding how to spend our lives. In the case of Lazarus, Jesus waited for four days before He went to see Mary and Martha. The woman with the issue of blood was healed immediately. Some blind men were healed immediately. In all these, there is the need for us as Christians to be sensitive to the Holy Spirit to know when and where to act. The Lord orders the steps of the righteous. The story of the Good Samaritan in Luke 10:30-37 explains it best.

We are told that both the Priest and the Levite went past the wounded man who had fallen victim to robbers and was badly wounded. They were probably in a hurry to go to church. The question is, which of the two situations was urgent and important? The church they were in a hurry to go was important but it didn't appear to be urgent. Conversely, the situation of the dying man was critically urgent and important. Sometimes, however, it is not easy to tell the urgent from the important. We therefore need the direction of the Holy Spirit in every decision we make.

Benefits of good time management

With good time management skills, you gain the following:

- You are in control of your time, your life, your stress and energy levels.
- You make progress at work.
- You are able to maintain a balance between work, personal and family activities.
- You have flexibility to respond to surprises or new opportunities.

6. *Financial Empowerment*

"Money answereth all things," says the Bible. God has indicated that in blessing, He will bless us, and in multiplying, He will multiply us. Having said this, it is important as a Christian Woman to be financially comfortable and secured. Ideally, every human being deserves to attain a decent level of financial security, but this does not always appear to be the case. Nonetheless, the Bible indicates that having financial wealth answers many of life's problems.

> *"A feast is made for laughter and wine makes life merry, and money is the answer for everything."*
>
> *(Ecclesiastes 10:19, NIV)*

Wealth refers to an abundance of items of economic value, or the state of controlling or possessing such items. It encompasses money, real estate, personal property, etc.

Financial independence is the ability to sustain one's lifestyle, if one chooses not to work or earn wages or salary. Who says money is not important? Life is not all about money but almost everything physical can be answered with money. Money gives us the ability to do more things and achieve our goals. In fact, money can make the marriage relationship better.

The key questions to ask are:

- Are savings and investments important?
- Is one's pension enough to live on?
- Will your children be able to meet all your financial needs in future?
- There is a time for everything.
- What are you doing with the time and opportunities to generate more income now?

> *"Lazy hands make for poverty, but diligent hands bring wealth. He who gathers crops in summer is a prudent son, but he who sleeps during harvest is a disgraceful son."*
>
> *(Proverbs 10:4-5, NIV)*
>
> *"Wealth gained by dishonesty will be diminished, but he who gathers by labor will increase."*
>
> *(Proverbs 13:11, NKJV)*

Napoleon Hill, the famous American author of 'Think and Grow Rich,' wrote: "Anybody can wish for riches, and most people do, but only a few know that a definite plan, plus a burning desire for wealth are the only dependable means of accumulating wealth." The road to wealth creation is through saving and investing.

Saving is the practice of setting aside a part of one's earnings today, regardless of how small. The aim of saving money is to prepare for a rainy day. There are surprises in life and a prudent woman is the one who always puts some money aside for the future. Do not be discouraged by the little savings you make because little drops of water make a mighty ocean. If you want to build wealth over the long haul, the only real solution is to invest. When you invest money, you have the opportunity to make more money through profits, interest, returns and dividends. You should not be a slave to money by constantly toiling day and night to make money. Rather, let your money work for you by learning smart and ingenious ways to make wealth.

Reasons to invest

- Life's unpredictable circumstances.
- Inadequate pension.
- Preparation towards retirement.
- To leave an inheritance for your children.
- To enable you to give your children a good education.
- To be a blessing to the body of Christ.
- To open an avenue for God to bless you.
- To be a virtuous woman and a wife of wisdom.

The rich buy assets while the poor and middle class buy liabilities and erroneously call them assets. An asset is anything that puts money in your pocket. A liability is anything that takes money out of your pocket. First, build assets such as financial investments and tangible properties and allow the returns to buy you the luxuries you desire. The golden rule is to be mindful of your expenditure and spend less than you earn.

Guidelines for savings and investments

- Open a savings account at a reputable financial

services institution, e.g. bank, insurance company or cooperative credit union. Compare interest rates and check for hidden fees.

- Set up a Standing Order or Direct Debit into a Savings Account.
- Ensure you save a minimum of 20% of your income every month after tithing.
- Avoid borrowing to start a business when the interest is high.
- If you are a trader or business person, ensure that you give yourself a salary and save part of it. Do not spend all your profit.
- Take a life endowment policy.
- Buying things on credit may be appropriate for some things, but consider the interest on it. The best recommendation is to save to buy.

Guidelines for effective housekeeping

- Create a monthly budget.
- Use a shopping list. Avoid impulse buying and as much as possible adhere to your budget.
- Compare prices before taking certain decisions to buy. Change brands and providers if need be.

- Make bulk purchases.

- Plan your menu. This will minimise the frequency of eating out. You could even prepare what you want to eat out.

- Avoid overcooking. Dish and store food in smaller quantities to avoid frequent reheating, which results in spoilage and wastage.

- Take advantage of the deep freezer. You can freeze food for up to three months.

- Spend less than you earn.

Key Learning Points

- *Your husband and family are within your 20% bracket. They need the bulk of your time.*

- *The time you set aside for your husband and family should be one deliberately created especially for them.*

- *The race that is set before you must be run within time.*

- *Manage your time as you would manage your money.*

- *As much as possible, try to create quality time for your husband and family.*

- *Do not give your husband time because you are free. Create the time and be with your husband and family as well as those in your 20% bracket.*

- *The time you spend with your husband and family should not be an incidental or accidental one but one deliberately created especially for them.*

- *Look for additional income no matter how small.*

- *Invest in instruments that appreciate in value as much as possible, such as land, property and gold.*

06

MANAGING MARITAL CHALLENGES

The trials and tribulations that sometimes confront us are so testing and worrying that we do not seem to have hope or faith that God will see us through them. Abraham waited 25 years from the time God promised him a son until the day the promise was fulfilled. Therefore, as Christian Women, when we are faced with challenges and there are compelling reasons to take certain decisions, it will be necessary for us to be patient and hopeful.

> *"When God made his promise to Abraham, since there was no one greater for him to swear by, he swore by himself, saying, 'I will surely bless you and give you many descendants.' And so after waiting patiently, Abraham received what was promised."*
>
> *(Hebrews 6:13–15, NIV)*

God will always make a way out of the challenges, for He has said in 1 Corinthians 10:13 (NIV): ***No temptation has overtaken you except what is common*** *to mankind. And God is faithful; he will not let you be tempted beyond what you can bear. But when you are tempted, he will also provide a way out so that you can endure it."*

Some common challenges

- Delayed marriage
- Difficulty in conception, and having children
- Children born with disability
- Children on drugs
- Children not doing well in school
- Husbands not providing adequately for the home
- Husbands not treating wives with understanding and honour
- In-law issues
- Business and job difficulties
- Sicknesses
- Fear of the future
- Financial insufficiency and debt

You may be reading this book right now and may be on the verge of taking a certain decision, which you know is not the best for you and your family but you seem to have no other option. I encourage you to take heart. Do not give up. Do not lose trust and confidence. God is saying to you, "Be Patient."

> *"I am the Lord, the God of all mankind. Is anything too hard for me?"*
>
> *(Jeremiah 32:27, NIV)*

> *"For the vision is yet for an appointed time; but at the end it shall speak, and it will not lie. Though it tarries, wait for it; because it will surely come, it will not tarry."*
>
> *(Habakkuk 2:3, NKJV)*

The prophet Habakkuk was worried that God did not protect His children. He asked God so many questions and God gave him the answer above. You may also be disappointed in one way or the other but what God is saying to you is that the vision will surely be realised. No matter how long it tarries it will surely come, so have faith and wait for it.

*"God is not human, that he should lie, not
a human being, that he should change his
mind. Does he speak and then not act?
Does he promise and not fulfill?"*

(Numbers 23:19, NIV)

Faithful is He who has called you and He will do it, for with God all things are possible.

Principles of waiting

- Be patient.

- Keep on praying in expectation.

- Keep on believing that God will do it.

- Do not give in to that man or that woman who could lead you astray.

- Have self-control in all things and at all times.

- Do not transgress to get what you want because it will be a bad deal and will not take you far.

Remember that the plans God has for us are plans for good and not for evil, plans that will lead us to an expected end.

When you have waited and have been obedient to God, the breakthrough will happen. This is what the sovereign Lord says: "*...None of My words will be delayed any longer, whatever I say will be fulfilled declares the Sovereign Lord". Ezekiel 12:28 (NIV)*

The marriage will come from God. The jobs will come from God because He gives us the power to make money. Deuteronomy 8:18 (NIV) says: *"But Remember the Lord your God, for it is he who gives you the ability to produce wealth...."*

The children will come from God.
"Behold, children are a gift of the Lord, the fruit of the womb is a reward." (Psalm 127:3, NASB)

The healing will come because *"He sent forth His Word and healed [us] and delivered [us] from [our] destruction." (Psalm 107:20, NASB)*

> *"I will make rivers flow on barren heights and springs within the valleys.*
> *I will turn the desert into pools of water*

and the parched ground into springs. I will put in the desert the cedar and the acacia, the myrtle and the olive. I will set junipers in the wasteland, the fir and the cypress together, so that people may see and know, may consider and understand, that the hand of the Lord has done this, that the Holy One of Israel has created it."

(Isaiah 41:18-20, NIV)

Key Learning Points

- *Be aggressive in the things of God.*
- *Continue to persevere.*
- *Continue to do good.*
- *Continue to pay your tithe.*
- *Continue to work in the house of God.*
- *Do not compromise; stay focused.*
- *But do not be entangled in sin, for He makes all things beautiful in His own time.*
- *Patience and endurance are our sustaining force.*

07

PERSONAL WALK WITH GOD

My education in the United Kingdom exposed the weakness in my relationship with the Holy Spirit. When I was writing my professional banking examination, a particular paper posed a huge challenge to me. I had a difficulty passing that paper. It was the only paper hindering my return to my motherland, Ghana.

Then one afternoon, a friend by name Dorcas Amoafo called me as I was preparing to write this particular paper again. She told me that the Lord had told her to tell me that I had not involved the Holy Spirit in my life as I ought to have done. This came as a surprise to me because at the very least, I operated in some of the gifts of the Holy Spirit.

I therefore asked her what she meant. For over thirty minutes on the phone, Dorcas started sharing with me the power and role of the Holy Spirit in our lives. She told me how intimate she was with the Holy Spirit to the extent that even if she had misplaced something in her home or in her office, she would ask the Holy Spirit to show her where it was. She gave me so many instances where the Holy Spirit had come to her and aided her.

She advised me to allow the Holy Spirit to choose the examination questions for me and deliberately ask Him what to study. At the end of the discussion, I repented before the Lord as I realised how I had not involved the Holy Spirit in my life as I ought to. John 16:13 (NIV) says: ***"But when he, the Spirit of truth, comes, he will guide you into all the truth…"***

In the end, I passed my exams after consciously involving the Holy Spirit in the preparation and writing of the exams. Since then, I have consciously involved the Holy Spirit in my life. I remember one time when I needed to get some documents to my husband who was in the USA at the time. He told me where the documents were but I searched for them in all the places that I needed to look but could not find them. I quickly remembered that I needed to ask the Holy Spirit to show me where the documents were. Soon after that, I found the documents in an obscure place where under normal circumstances I would not have looked.

There was also another time when I was driving in the city of Accra, Ghana, and was locked up in such a heavy traffic jam that it was literally the survival of the fittest. I just did not know what to do. But just then I remembered there was a friend that was closer than a brother. I quickly asked the Holy Spirit to help me out. Soon, the car ahead of me moved a few feet and stopped for one reason or the other. This created the perfect opportunity for me to move on. It was simply awesome.

In situations that I cannot handle at home, I just ask the Holy Spirit to take control and He does it very well. It has been so amazing because He has become part of me. One of the secrets to a successful marriage relationship is the daily deliberate involvement of the Holy Spirit in your marriage. Whether it is financial, social, emotional or psychological stress, we need the Holy Spirit to boost our resolve.

Sometimes certain situations arise for which ordinarily I expect my husband to get upset, but the reaction is positive when I ask the Holy Spirit to take over. The complexities of marriage life are now so enormous that our human capabilities and capacities alone cannot handle them. We need help and the Holy Spirit is our helper.

Our good Lord has commissioned us to shine as light and bring transformation to the darkness that sometimes engulfs us. Let us look at some of the effects of light. Light is beneficial, light radiates, and light shines within a particular radius. Light enables you to see ahead in order to make an informed decision as there may be roadblocks on the way. Light is a source of strength as it gives you the upper hand. Our lights need to shine.

> *"Arise, shine, for your light has come, and*
> *the glory of the Lord rises upon you."*
> *(Isaiah 60:1, NIV)*

We are also the salt of the earth. Salt has powerful properties. A little speck of salt changes the taste of food. It gives food a better taste. The secret to a successful marriage relationship is to be true light and salt.

Godly character

Godly character is the evidence of a redeemed life. When a defense lawyer wants to win a case, he makes every attempt to discredit the evidence against his client. This sometimes means attacking the evidence so vigorously that in the end it is destroyed and no longer reliable. Satan cannot destroy the truth of Christ's resurrection and victory over evil so he goes after the evidence. A godly character is the evidence of Christ's resurrection. Satan will come after your character with a passion to seek to destroy it.

Character is the quality that makes an individual. Decency, self-control, integrity in what we do and say, both publicly and privately, give evidence of Christ's influence in our lives. The more Christ shines through you, the more His kingdom is established on earth. Lying, gossiping and backbiting are evidence of a life controlled by Satan. This is not what Christ has called us to do. Each time we do these things, Satan laughs at us and exalts himself at such victory.

We need to come to a realisation as Christians that there is more at stake than our own little names when we act as those who have no reason to live with integrity. Each time you are tempted to compromise your stand and character as a Christian, a battle is going on. Imagine what would happen if all Christians started living an honest life and their 'no' meant 'no' and their 'yes' meant 'yes.' Imagine the influence you would possess if people around you could rely on your word as the truth and your character as reliable. You would do more to propagate the gospel of Christ than many words could accomplish.

When you say you will do something, do it. When you allow the character of Christ to influence your life, it will inhibit the control the world has over you. People will start to take notice of you. You will start to have an influence over them. God will also entrust you with His power and gifts because you can handle them and your character will prevent any abuse of your gifts.

Character is the balance of power. Once we get a revelation of the importance of godly character, it will be easier for Christ to trust us with true riches.

All our decisions and actions in life are rooted in our character. Look in the mirror of God's Word and embrace His character. There is a lot at stake when we do not develop our character.

Forgiveness

The world is full of betrayal and disappointment. As emotional beings, we easily get hurt, and become bitter by the intentional or unintentional actions of our husbands, children and those around us and this can lead to unforgiveness if not checked.

Though a Christian, Spirit-filled and a preacher of the Word, I had a mental catalogue of all the things that my husband had done to me at one time or the other. I pondered over them, made some meaning out of them and felt extremely justified for not being happy with him. The act of cataloguing those offences made me sinful in the eyes of God. The Bible admonishes us to forgive when we are wronged, and to keep no record of wrongs.

According to the dictionary, 'to forgive' is to cease to

feel resentment against an offender, that is, to pardon one's enemies. Forgiveness can be a challenge for several reasons when the person who wronged us does not seem to deserve our forgiveness.

But I have come to realise that forgiveness is especially essential and critical in marriage. We should learn to forgive one another so that we can walk in the purposes of God and grow in our relationship with one another. I want us to view forgiveness from the perspective of tolerance. I remember when my husband travelled outside Ghana for a few years, it was quite a challenge managing the home and our children, as my job required that I travelled a lot. It became a real issue because, to a large extent, he was not comfortable with my frequent travels.

It got to a time when telling him that I was about to travel always put fear in me. It was an emotionally and psychologically stressful time for me. I almost decided to do something very silly "choose my job over my marriage". I needed liberty. I could not tell anybody what I was nurturing in my mind because people knew us and really respected us.

I was a marriage counselor but I thought I needed freedom. I was adamant in my heart and determined to go ahead with my plans, but my problem was how to embark on it. I reflected on the situation when Joseph wanted to put Mary away and was thinking about how to do it. At that time, we had been married for about thirteen years and had had all our children.

Then I had a dream. In the dream, I was lying down and all of a sudden, I saw a huge man walk towards me. He held a big, white, well-ironed bed sheet. Then he opened the bed sheet wide with his two hands from end to end. This should tell you how huge he was and how long his hands were. I think this scene resonates with the word of the Lord in Isaiah 59:1 (NKJV). "...*The Lord's hand is not shortened, that it cannot save. Nor His ear heavy, that it cannot hear.*"

At one corner of the bed sheet was a small black stain. The huge man presented the bed sheet to me, but I told him I did not want it because it had a little stain in it. Then the man said: "this small black stain is nothing to make you refuse this lovely bed sheet." I insisted that I did not like the bed sheet. Disappointed, the huge man turned and said, "learn to tolerate the weaknesses of people." And I suddenly woke up from the dream.

In the morning, the dream replayed in my mind repeatedly. I was still thinking about how to go about my unwise decision. Then when I went to church, my spiritual father Archbishop Nicholas Duncan-Williams, founder of Action Chapel International, said that he wanted to pray for marriages and marital issues. As he prayed the dream came back to me again and, suddenly, I heard a question in my spirit: "who do you share your bed sheet with?" I immediately asked myself, "whom could I possibly share my bed sheet with?"

Then it dawned on me that it is my husband. I then realised that my husband was the one who was shown to me in the dream. He had a little dark spot. He was imperfect but in totality he had a good heart and yet I was not appreciative. I remembered what the huge man told me in the dream, "learn to accept and tolerate the weaknesses of people."I repented immediately and realised that I was being selfish and judgmental. There and then, I repented from those gloomy thoughts and was liberated from what had been putting me down.

What I am trying to share with women and for that matter all married partners is that, we should be tolerant with each other. What I was contemplating was not in the will of God, but I was determined to put the will of God aside just to satisfy my personal desires. The dream made me realise that I had taken a decision that had incriminated me already. I was just trying to portray to everyone that I was the perfect one but that was not the case. Our husbands may not be justified in some things they do but we should be charitable and accommodating. God has an eye on our marriages and He knows whatever goes on.

A philosopher once said: "Be to her virtues very kind, be to her faults a little blind." This adage is a guide to all marriage couples since no person is infallible. Unforgivingness is a spirit that can easily hold us back from walking in the purposes and will of God.

The following scriptures should be our guiding principles.

> *"So I say, walk by the Spirit, and you will not gratify the desires of the flesh. For the flesh desires what is contrary to the Spirit, and the Spirit what is contrary to the flesh. They are in conflict with each other, so that you are not to do whatever you want. But if you are led by the Spirit, you are not under the law."*
>
> *(Galatians 5:16-18, NIV)*

> *"Get rid of all bitterness, rage and anger, brawling and slander, along with every form of malice. Be kind and compassionate to one another, forgiving each other, just as in Christ God forgave you."*
>
> *(Ephesians 4:31-32, NIV)*

"Therefore, as God's chosen people, holy and dearly loved, clothe yourselves with compassion, kindness, humility, gentleness and patience. Bear with each other and forgive one another if any of you has a grievance against someone. Forgive as the Lord forgave you. And over all these virtues put on love, which binds them all together in perfect unity. Let the peace of Christ rule in your hearts, since as members of one body you were called to peace. And be thankful. Let the message of Christ dwell among you richly as you teach and admonish one another with all wisdom through psalms, hymns, and songs from the Spirit, singing to God with gratitude in your hearts. And whatever you do, whether in word or deed, do it all in the name of the Lord Jesus, giving thanks to God the Father through him."

(Colossians 3:12-17, NIV)

God knows we have been wronged. He knows we have been hurt. He knows the pain and the disappointment, yet He tells us to forgive because forgiveness puts us in a right relationship with Him. 1John 4:20 (ESV) tells us: *"If anyone says, 'I love God,' and hates his brother, he is a liar; for he who does not love his brother whom he has seen cannot love God whom he has not seen."* You cannot have it both ways. Loving God means loving others, which includes granting and seeking forgiveness.

Secondly, forgiving others removes any roadblocks to your prayers. Mark 11:25 (ESV) says: *"And whenever you stand praying, forgive, if you have anything against anyone, so that your Father also who is in heaven may forgive you your trespasses."*

Thirdly, forgiving others ensures that God forgives you. Matthew 6:14-15 (NKJV) says: *"For if you forgive men their trespasses, your heavenly Father will also forgive you. But if you do not forgive men their trespasses, neither will your Father forgive your trespasses."* When God has forgiven you of so much, why should He not expect you to forgive others also generously?

A fourth benefit is found in 1 Timothy 1:5 (ESV): *"The aim of our charge is love that issues from a pure heart and a good conscience and a sincere faith."* Real love comes from a good conscience; it means you have taken care of business with God. There is no barrier between you and Him. Nothing makes you feel guilty or ashamed to approach Him. Having real love means you forgive when you should and ask Him for forgiveness when it is necessary to do so.

Lastly, forgiveness leads to personal and spiritual renewal and improves our relationship with others as it frees us from the hurt and anger that may be gaining root in our lives.

Benefits of forgiveness

- We walk in obedience of the word of God and as a result, God blesses us.
- We demonstrate to the world that we are indeed children of God. "By their fruit, ye shall know them".

- God revenges on our behalf. He lays a table in the presence of our enemies.
- Our sins are forgiven 'Forgive us our sins as we forgive those who trespass against us.'
- We are emotionally and psychologically healed and liberated.
- We do not give the devil a foothold in our hearts.
- God hears our prayers.
- Our bodies can accommodate the Spirit of God.
- The Spirit of God is at work in our lives.

As Christian Women, it is important that we pray for the following:

- God to empty us of every pain and hurt.
- The Holy Spirit to remind us of any pain we are harbouring.
- The Holy Spirit to heal us of pain and hurt.
- The Holy Spirit to give us the spirit to love our enemies.
- The Holy Spirit to dwell in us.

Godliness

Godliness avoids anything that brings disunity or division in the church. It lives unselfishly, making others the primary focus of its concerns. Ephesians 5:22 (NIV) admonishes that: ***"Wives submit yourself to your own husband as to the Lord."*** Women are not made inferior to men. They are designed to be help meets.

The fruit of the Holy Spirit is to be nurtured in our lives every day. Only the Holy Spirit can produce these fruits. We cannot do this on our own effort. The first three of the fruits concern our Love towards God. The next three deal with social relationship. The last three describe principles that should guide the conduct of a Christian.

"But the fruit of the Spirit is love, joy, peace, patience, kindness, goodness, faithfulness, gentleness and self-control. Against such things there is no law. Those who belong to Christ Jesus have crucified the sinful nature with its passions and

desires. Since we live by the Spirit, let us keep in step with the spirit. Let us not become conceited, provoking and envying each other."

(Galatians 5:22-26, NIV)

"Wives, in the same way submit yourselves to your own husbands so that, if any of them do not believe the word, they may be won over without words by the behavior of their wives, when they see the purity and reverence of your lives."

(1 Peter 3:1-2, NIV)

Key Learning Points

- *God is interested in our marriages.*
- *Let us be patient and tolerant with our husbands, for we are as fallible as they are.*
- *Their fallibility is the reason we were created to be help meets to them.*
- *Always walk in forgiveness.*

08

LIVING A FULFILLED CHRISTIAN LIFE

The contented Christian Woman is one who is at peace with herself irrespective of what goes on around her, whether good or bad. She is confident in herself because she has confidence in God.

She believes all is well. She believes all will be well.

In 2 Kings 4:8-37 we learn about the Shunamite Woman.

Profile of the Shunamite Woman

- She was a wealthy woman.
- She recognised and respected the ministry of Elisha.
- She consulted her husband and provided Elisha not only with a room but everything else that he needed: bed, table, chair and a lamp stand. She used her substance to bless the man of God.
- She had a crucial need, a need that can be a great worry to many married women, she did not have a child. What made her situation almost hopeless was that her husband was old.
- In spite of her need, she did not throw a pity

party or complain. She was rather contented and hopeful.

In fact, she did not even go to Elisha first to petition her need. Elisha asked her, "What can I do for you?" Her answer was, "I dwell among my own people." This means I am comfortable I do not have a need. I do not need anything, I am okay. Rather, Gehazi revealed that she did not have a child.

She became pregnant and had a son. The child grew up but one day died unexpectedly. She went up, laid him on the bed of Elisha, and shut the door. She called her husband and said I need one young man and one donkey that I may run to the man of God. Her husband asked why she wanted to go and see Elisha, as it was neither the Sabbath nor the New Moon. Her answer was "It is well." She did not tell the servant either.

On her arrival, Elisha sent Gehazi to ask her if it was well with her, her husband or her son. Her answer was "it is well."

What the Shunamite woman did not do

- She did not panic.
- She did not shout or scream.
- She did not go about telling people "my child is dead."
- She did not lose confidence in God.

The Shunamite woman is the epitome of the contented Christian Woman, a woman of great faith.

Attributes of a contented woman

- Inner Joy
- Peace
- Self control
- Confidence
- Generous in Prayer, gifts and the work of God
- Sees God as the source of everything
- Has expectations
- Has self value
- Purposeful
- Focused

As Christians, we should walk confidently in faith knowing that our God will supply all our needs according to His riches in Glory by Christ Jesus and that nothing will be able to separate us from the love of Christ.

"So do not throw away your confidence: it will be richly rewarded."

(Hebrews 10:35, NIV)

"But seek first his kingdom and his righteousness, and all these things will be given to you as well."

(Mathew 6:33, NIV)

You may be reading this book and you may be waiting on God for a husband, a child, a job, healing or restoration for your marriage. Please, know one thing your God is a faithful God and He will keep in perfect peace those whose mind are focused on Him. The plans He has for us are plans for good and not for evil to give us hope and a future. You will also say "it is well" because we live by faith and not by sight.

Key Learning Points

- *Life without challenges ceases to be life.*

- *Marital challenges are as normal as labour pains.*

- *What we feed on grows. Feeding challenges with negativity will yield negative results and vice versa.*

- *God is a faithful God who will not tempt or test you beyond what you can take. He will always make away of escape.*

- *Our God is still on the throne.*

09

NUGGETS FOR
MARRIED COUPLES

You might be surprised to learn that some of the best ways for improving your marriage are based on simple acts and deeds.

Show courtesy

Start by showing your husband courtesy. This may seem easy to do, but couples easily fall out of the habit of showing one another the same common courtesy they show the bank teller or the cashier at the grocery store. Courtesy makes your spouse feel worthy of your respect.

No matter how long you have been married, saying 'please' and 'thank you' will never go out of style and neither will greeting your partner pleasantly and acknowledging his or her presence. You probably did so when your marriage was new, but what happened? Always remember that making someone feel special, cared for and worthy inspires that person to reciprocate.

Intimate communication

If you want to develop a more intimate marriage

relationship, engage in communication that is intimate. It is necessary to be open and honest with your thoughts and feelings. Additionally, strive to be a good or active listener rather than a passive or a combative listener.

Plan some fun together

It is easy to get caught up with everyday life and forget about being together. A partner can then become disappointed or displeased if there is no quality time shared together. Take the time to enjoy your spouse, your love as you did earlier in your marriage.

Make sure you plan some time together doing activities that you both enjoy and do this as often as possible. It does not really matter what you choose to do as long as you enjoy doing it together. Having fun together will enrich the relationship.

Minimal Expectations

Another step to take to improve a marriage is to have minimal expectations of your spouse.

Earlier, I shared with you those fantastic expectations I had of my marriage and how those expectations were dashed to some extent. I ignored our various individual backgrounds and upbringing and was expecting to experience what I was used to experiencing from my background. The good news is that your expectations can grow with the relationship after knowing each other much better.

Set goals together

All relationships, whether family or work related, need to have something to look forward to. It is important as a couple to discuss some of the goals that you would like to achieve in the coming years. Look five years, ten years, and twenty years ahead and set some realistic and attainable goals. If you write them down they are more likely to happen. Also, this planning can help you save up for some of the important activities you want to accomplish in life.

Put on a smile

When times are tough in a relationship, it is much

easier to be angry and put up a wall. Sometimes this is the worst action a person can take in a relationship. Instead, consider smiling through it all and work together to figure out the problem. It could just be a phase that will eventually pass. Also remember that if one spouse has a smile on, the other is more apt to put one on as well. The Bible tells us to *"count it all joy, my brethren, when you meet various trials"* (James 1:2, RSV). So, even in the midst of trial and tribulation, let your joy remain.

Positive thinking

We have all heard it before but focusing on the positive can really improve a person's mood as well as his relationship as a whole. Being around people who frequently focus on the negative aspects of marriage can breed cancer in your own marriage. It is important to have friends who appreciate their spouses and enjoy spending time with them. Have positive thoughts about your spouse. The Bible indicates in Philippians 4:8 (NIV): *"Finally, brothers and sisters, whatever is true, whatever is noble, whatever is right, whatever is pure, whatever is lovely, whatever is admirable if anything is excellent or praiseworthy think about such things."*

Pray and share the Word of God Together

It is important that as a couple you cultivate the habit of praying and sharing the Word of God together. As a couple, you form a quorum to achieve so much. The Bible says, one shall put a thousand to flight and two shall put ten thousand to flight. If two shall agree on anything according to His will, it shall be established.

Key Learning Points

- *The little things in marriage make a lot of difference and add a lot of spice to the relationship.*

- *The courtesies of life should not be limited to those outside the family but should rather commence from our homes.*

- *Remaining positive, both in thought, disposition and attitude will always oil the wheels of the marriage.*

CONCLUSION

God is faithful and He wishes above all things that we should prosper and be in good health as our souls prosper. His intention is to make our marriage relationships as sweet as wine. He will therefore never tempt us beyond what we can take, but in every temptation He will make a way of escape for us.

A Woman is a Woman

As women we have strategic roles to play in the purposes of God. The qualities of a woman are still embedded in her irrespective of her state. There is a woman and a wife in every woman. When God created the world He said it was good.

Genesis 2:15 (KJV) says,

> *"And the LORD God took the man, and put him into the garden of Eden to dress it and to keep it."*

Though, God had created a perfect world, in Genesis 2:18 (NKJV), He recognised a problem in the garden.

And the Lord God said, "It is not good that man should be alone; I will make him a helper comparable to him."

One critical observation I have made is that, after God had created everything, He said it was good but God made the statement 'It is not good for a man to live alone' ONLY AFTER He had given man the responsibility of dressing the garden and keeping it.

This clearly implies that:

- Men do not have everything it takes to dress the garden and keep it.
- Men are deficient in certain things.
- Men cannot dress and keep the garden alone.
- If men had it all, they would not have needed the support of women to accomplish the task.
- God needs the support of women to enable men accomplish their purpose.
- God has given women what it takes to support men to be complete.
- Women have a strategic position in the plan of God.

God in His own wisdom has deposited in women some qualities that men do not have hence, God's direction for women to support their husbands.

God's expectations of the Christian Woman inside and outside of marriage are all encapsulated in Proverbs 31:10-31.

There is a virtue in every woman and we can all rise up to the occasion just as women like Rahab, Hannah, Esther, Deborah, the Shunamite Woman and many others did to make a difference. We can emulate their examples and make a difference in our marriages, community and sphere of influence.

Rabab

Rahab displayed untold womanly qualities irrespective of her state which led to the victory of the Israelites over the people of Jericho.

Hannah Stood up.

"Once when they had finished eating and drinking in Shiloh, Hannah stood up...." (1Samuel 1:9, NIV)

Esther Stood up

"On the third day Esther put on her royal robes and stood in the inner court of the palace, in front of the king's hall…." (Esther 5:1, NIV)

Deborah Stood up

"Villagers in Israel would not fight; they held back until I, Deborah, arose, until I arose, a mother in Israel." (Judges 5:7, NIV)

The Shunamite woman

The Shunamite woman stood up when she lost her son and said, ***"I will not let my dream die, I will not let my glory die, I will not let my joy die."***

I thank God for the lives of women. I praise God for their enduring Spirit, for their selflessness and hard work.

> *"Arise, shine, for your light has come, and*
> *the glory of the Lord rises upon you."*
>
> *(Isaiah 60:1, NIV)*

May you be richly blessed

Recommended Scriptures

The scriptures below have helped me at various times to pray and I trust they will help you as well.

CONCERNING PROGRESS

I will give you every place where you set your foot, as I promised Moses.

(Joshua 1:3, NIV)

I will make rivers flow on barren heights and springs within the valleys. I will turn the desert into pools of water and the parched ground into springs. I will put in the desert the cedar and the acacia, the myrtle and the olive. I will set pines in the wasteland the fir and the cypress together, so that people may see and know and consider and understand that the hand of the Lord has done this that the Holy One of Israel has created it.

(Isaiah 41:18-20, NIV)

His divine power has given us everything we need for life and godliness through our knowledge of him who called us by his own glory and goodness.

(2 Peter 1:3, NIV)

Instead of your shame you will have a double portion, and instead of humiliation they will shout for joy over their portion. Therefore they will possess a double portion in their land, Everlasting joy will be theirs.

(Isaiah 61:7, NASB)

I took you from the ends of the earth, from the farthest corners I called you. I said, "You are my servant"; I have chosen you and have not rejected you. So do not fear, for I am with you; do not be dismayed, for I am your God. I will strengthen you and help you; I will uphold you with my righteous right hand. All who rage against you will surely be ashamed and disgraced; those who oppose you will be as nothing and perish. Though you search for your enemies, you will not find them. Those who wage war against you will be as nothing at all. For I am the Lord, your God who takes hold of your right hand and says to you, Do not fear; I will help you.

(Isaiah 41:9–13, NIV)

…Not by might nor by power, but by my Spirit, says the Lord Almighty.

(Zechariah 4:6, NIV)

I will give you the keys of the kingdom of heaven; whatever you bind on earth will be bound in heaven, and whatever you loose on earth will be loosed in heaven.

(Matthew 16:19, NIV)

These, then, are the things you should teach. Encourage and rebuke with all authority. Do not let anyone despise you.

(Titus 2:15, NIV)

May God of peace, who through the blood of the eternal covenant brought back from the dead our Lord Jesus... equip you with everything good for doing his will....

(Hebrews 13:20–21, NIV)

For with God nothing is ever impossible, and no word form God shall be without power or impossible of fulfillment.

(Luke 1:37, AMP)

CONCERNING JOY

You turned my wailing into dancing; you removed my sackcloth and clothed me with joy.

(Psalm 30:11, NIV)

Rejoice in the Lord always. I will say it again: Rejoice!

(Philippians 4:4, NIV)

Through Jesus, therefore, let us continually offer to God a sacrifice of praise—the fruit of lips that confess his name.

(Hebrews 13:15, NIV)

CONCERNING FEAR

Have I not commanded you? Be strong and courageous. Do not be terrified; do not be discouraged, for the Lord your God will be with you wherever you go.

(Joshua 1:9, NIV)

The Lord said to Joshua, 'Do not be afraid of them; I have given them into your hand. Not one of them will be able to withstand you.'

(Joshua10:8, NIV)

The eternal God is your refuge, and underneath are the everlasting arms. He will drive out your enemy before you, saying, 'Destroy him!'

(Deuteronomy 33:27, NIV)

...No weapon forged against you will prevail, and you will refute every tongue that accuses you. This is the heritage of the servants of the Lord, and this is their vindication from me, declares the Lord.

(Isaiah 54:17, NIV)

Before they call I will answer, while they are still speaking I will hear.

(Isaiah 65:24, NIV)

If you remain in me and my words remain in you, ask whatever you wish, and it will be given you. This is to my Father's glory, that you bear much fruit, showing yourselves to be my disciples.

(John 15:7-8, NIV)

But thanks be to God! He gives us the victory through our Lord Jesus Christ.

(1 Corinthians 15:57, NIV)

"For I know the plans I have for you," declares the Lord, "plans to prosper you and not to harm you, plans to give you hope and a future."

(Jeremiah 29:11, NIV)

May the God of hope fill you with all joy and peace as you trust in him, so that you may overflow with hope by the power of the Holy Spirit.

(Romans 15:13, NIV)

Do not be afraid of them; the Lord your God himself will fight for you.

(Deuteronomy 3:22, NIV)

But do not be afraid of them; remember well what the Lord your God did to Pharaoh and to all Egypt.

(Deuteronomy 7:18, NIV)

…This is what the Lord says to you: "Do not be afraid or discouraged because of this vast army. For the battle is not yours, but God's."

(2 Chronicles 20:15, NIV)

The fear of God came upon all the kingdoms of the countries when they heard how the Lord had fought against the enemies of Israel. And the kingdom of Jehoshaphat was at peace, for his God had given him rest on every side.

(2 Chronicles 20:29–30, NIV)

You will be protected from the lash of the tongue, and need not fear when destruction comes. You will laugh at destruction and famine, and need not fear the beasts of the earth.

(Job 5:21–22, NIV)

But you are a shield around me, O Lord; you bestow glory on me and lift up my head…I will not fear the tens of thousands drawn up against me on every side.

(Psalm 3:3, 6, NIV)

Even though I walk through the valley of the shadow of death, I will fear no evil, for you are with me; your rod and your staff, they comfort me.

(Psalm 23:4, NIV)

The Lord is my light and my salvation— whom shall I fear?
The Lord is the stronghold of my life—of whom shall I be afraid?

(Psalm 27:1, NIV)

CONCERNING PEACE

You will keep in perfect peace him whose mind is steadfast, because he trusts in you.

(Isaiah 26:3, NIV)

Peace I leave with you; my peace I give you. I do not give to you as the world gives. Do not let your hearts be troubled and do not be afraid.

(John 14:27, NIV)

I have told you these things, so that in me you may have peace. In this world you will have trouble. But take heart! I have overcome the world.

(John 16:33, NIV)

So do not fear, for I am with you; do not be dismayed, for I am your God. I will strengthen you and help you; I will uphold you with my righteous right hand.

(Isaiah 41:10, NIV)

But now, this is what the Lord says— he who created you, O Jacob, he who formed you O Israel: "Fear not, for I have redeemed you; I have summoned you by name; you are mine."

(Isaiah 43:1, NIV)

…If God is for us, who can be against us?

(Romans 8:31, NIV)

For I am convinced that neither death nor life, neither angels nor demons, neither the present nor the future, nor any powers, neither height nor depth, nor anything else in all creation, will be able to separate us from the love of God that is in Christ Jesus our Lord.

(Romans 8:38–39, NIV)

For God did not give us a spirit of timidity, but a spirit of power, of love and of self-discipline.

(2 Timothy 1:7, NIV)

So we say with confidence, "the Lord is my helper; I will not be afraid. What can man do to me?"

(Hebrews 13:6, NIV)

If you suffer, it should not be as a murderer or thief or any other kind of criminal, or even as a meddler. However, if you suffer as a Christian, do not be ashamed, but praise God that you bear that name.

(1 Peter 4:15-16, NIV)

The Lord will fulfill his purpose for me…

(Psalm 138:8, NIV)

Many are the plans in a man's heart, but it is the Lord's purpose that prevails.

(Proverbs 19:21, (NIV)

He who fears the Lord has a secure fortress, and for his children it will be a refuge.

(Proverbs 14:26, NIV)

…I will contend with those who contend with you, and your children I will save.

(Isaiah 49:25, NIV)

And God is able to make all grace abound toward you, so that in all things at all times, chaving all that you need, you will abound in every good work.

(2 Corinthians 9:8, NIV)

NOTES

NOTES

NOTES